W9-CRY-335

TOP 10
SPORTS
★STARS★

FOOTBALL'S
TOP
10 RUNNING
BACKS

Barry Wilner

Enslow Publishers, Inc.
40 Industrial Road
Box 398
Berkeley Heights, NJ 07922
USA

http://www.enslow.com

ACKNOWLEDGMENTS

The author would like to thank Andrea Adelson, Nancy Armour, Jaime Aron, Larry Lage, Bernie Wilson, and Tom Withers for their help with this book.

• •

DEDICATION

To Helene, my Hall of Famer.

Library of Congress Cataloging-in-Publication Data

Wilner, Barry.
   Football's top 10 running backs / Barry Wilner.
      p. cm. — (Top 10 sports stars)
   Includes bibliographical references and index.
   Summary: "A collective biography of the top 10 running backs, both past and present, which includes accounts of game action, career statistics, and more"—Provided by publisher.
   ISBN 978-0-7660-3468-6
   1. Running backs (Football)—United States—Biography—Juvenile literature.
   2. Running backs (Football)—Rating of—United States—Juvenile literature. I. Title.
   II. Title: Football's top ten running backs.
   GV939.A1W59 2010
   796.3320922—dc22
   [B]

                                             2009027171

Printed in the United States of America

052010 Lake Book Manufacturing, Inc., Melrose Park, IL

10 9 8 7 6 5 4 3 2 1

Illustration Credits: All images courtesy of the Associated Press/ Wide World Photos, except pp. 30, 33, courtesy of All-Pro Photography; and pp. 34 and 37, courtesy of Chris Hamilton Photography.

Cover Illustration: Associated Press/ Wide World Photos.

TOP 10

CONTENTS

Whether it has been Jim Brown plowing over defenders, Tony Dorsett scooting around them, or LaDainian Tomlinson leaping over them, running backs have been stars ever since the NFL began eight decades ago.

They tend to have different styles, but one thing that is the same is their desire to carry the ball often. It doesn't matter if their team is close to the opponent's end zone or stuck deep in its own territory, their motto is "Give me the ball and block for me."

There can be a beauty in how they go about their jobs. Think of Barry Sanders taking a pitchout, running wide, cutting behind his blockers, and speeding downfield like a racehorse coming down the stretch of the Kentucky Derby.

Or Eric Dickerson hurdling high over a pile of players at the goal line and soaring into the end zone.

There also can be breathtaking power, such as Jerome Bettis, perfectly nicknamed "The Bus," mowing down tacklers to gain those extra inches for a first down.

The great running backs, from the 1950s and '60s to the present day, get stronger as the game goes on. In the fourth quarter, when defensive players are exhausted, the guys toting the ball are at their best.

Brown, Bettis, and Franco Harris were as much fullbacks as halfbacks, using their bulk and strength to dominate. Sanders might have been the most slippery runner ever. Dickerson used long strides in an upright style that invited tacklers to make big hits on him; they rarely could.

Curtis Martin was as steady as they come, churning out 1,000-yard season after 1,000-yard season. So was Emmitt Smith, the career rushing leader and a three-time Super Bowl winner.

Walter Payton is considered the model for the modern back: tough, relentless, always prepared.

Each of the stars in Top 10 Running Backs was a record-setter during his career. Bettis, Brown, Dorsett, Harris, Payton, and Smith were leaders on NFL championship teams. All of them either are in the Pro Football Hall of Fame or should be someday.

Is it any wonder that football coaches from high school to the pros insist the main road to success is, well, staying on the road—running the ball?

JEROME BETTIS

JEROME
BETTIS

Jerome Bettis wanted to take his Steelers teammates on a "Bus" ride, from Pittsburgh to his hometown, Detroit. All the way to the 2006 Super Bowl.

Bettis was given the nickname "The Bus" in college because a student reporter at Notre Dame wrote he ran over defenders like a bus. Now he was ready to end his thirteen-year NFL career. But he wanted to go out a winner.

"I'm going home," Bettis said after helping the Steelers beat the Broncos in the AFC Championship Game. "I'm going to my first Super Bowl, and it's in Motown."[1]

Growing up as the youngest of three children, Jerome lived in a poor neighborhood. Heading to school, he usually wore a white dress shirt, glasses, and a wide smile, and carried a tattered briefcase with a broken handle.

Jerome did not play organized football until he was in the ninth grade. Even though he had asthma, Jerome played defensive line and linebacker. Then his coach put him in the backfield. In his first two starts, he combined for 300 yards rushing and scored four touchdowns.

He was also a fine student, making the National Honor Society before heading to Notre Dame. Although he did not win any championships in college, Bettis was good enough to be drafted tenth overall in 1993 by the Rams.

"The first thing I bought when I signed my contract was a new house for my parents," he said.[2]

After two excellent seasons in Los Angeles, he was traded to Pittsburgh, where Bettis spent a decade as one of the NFL's top runners. He was always at his best close to the goal line, and when he drove the Steelers to the Super Bowl, Jerome ranked fifth in career yards rushing (13,662), tenth in touchdowns rushing (91), and first in popularity in Steel Town.

"I'm going to enjoy the time I spent with Jerome," said Super Bowl MVP Hines Ward. "We're sending Jerome out on a great note."[3]

That great note was his only championship. It meant everything to Bettis, who said his other biggest success was establishing The Bus Stops Here Foundation for underprivileged children.

"The script right now, if you took it to Hollywood they'd turn it down, saying it couldn't happen," Bettis said. "I've had a very special run."[4]

JEROME BETTIS

BORN: February 16, 1972, Detroit, Michigan.

HIGH SCHOOL: Mackenzie High School, Detroit, Michigan.

COLLEGE: Notre Dame University.

PRO: Los Angeles/ St. Louis Rams, 1993–1995; Pittsburgh Steelers, 1996–2005.

HONORS: Six Pro-Bowl Selections (1993, 1994, 1996, 1997, 2001, 2004).

JIM BROWN

JIM
BROWN

In late 1999, the Associated Press selected the player of the century in each sport. The hands-down winner in pro football was Jim Brown.

Although he played less than a decade for Cleveland, Brown made such an impact on the sport—and on anyone who tried to tackle him—that picking him not only as the best runner but the best overall player was easy.

Brown retired in 1965 to become a movie actor. When he entered the Hall of Fame in 1971, he held the record for yards rushing, with 12,312 in nine 12-game seasons. Walter Payton didn't break the mark until nineteen years after Brown's retirement, and Payton played in 16-game seasons.

"When someone tells me they've seen a great running back, I tell them, 'Go get tapes of Jim Brown. Then you've seen a great running back,'" said Oakland Raiders owner and former Coach Al Davis.[1]

In Brown's day, fullbacks often were the main running backs. At 6-foot-2, 235 pounds, Brown was as big as most linebackers, even some linemen. He was fast enough to run around them, but so powerful he often ran over defenders—or carried them on his back or clinging to his legs for yards at a time.

Giants linebacker Sam Huff spent years in college and the pros trying to tackle Brown, whom Huff called "the perfectly built human being."[2]

Once, Brown knocked Huff out cold during a collision on the field.

Many times after his powerful runs, Brown would get up slowly and walk back to the huddle. Was he hurt?

No way. On the next play, he would run just as hard.

Brown was a two-time NFL MVP, in 1957 as a rookie, and 1965. He also was the league's top rookie in '57—no one else has won rookie of the year and MVP in the same season.

He led the Browns to the 1964 NFL championship in an upset of Baltimore; in all, Brown played in three title contests, including a loss to Green Bay in 1965 that was his final NFL game.

Was he no longer a force by then? Actually, Brown had one of his best seasons in '65: 1,544 yards and 17 touchdowns in 12 games.

His most impressive season was 1963, with 1,863 yards rushing (an amazing 6.4 yards a carry).

In all, Brown led NFL rushers in eight of his nine seasons, gaining more than 1,000 yards in seven. He averaged an unmatched 5.22 yards a game.

JIM BROWN

BORN: February 17, 1936, St. Simons Island, Georgia.

HIGH SCHOOL: Manhasset High School, Manhasset, New York.

COLLEGE: Syracuse University.

PRO: Cleveland Browns, 1957–1965.

RECORDS: NFL Record for Career Touchdowns, 126 (106, Rushing; 20, Receiving).

HONORS: NFL Rookie of the Year, 1957. Pro Football Hall of Fame, 1971.

ERIC DICKERSON

ERIC
DICKERSON

No one has ever run away from

NFL defenders in his first two pro

seasons the way Eric Dickerson did.

An All-American at SMU and the second overall pick behind John Elway in the 1983 draft that produced six Hall of Famers in the first round, Dickerson set a rookie record with 1,808 yards rushing for the Los Angeles Rams. His second season was even more productive with 2,105 yards, the most anyone ever gained in one year.

His first season remains the most impressive in Dickerson's mind.

"As I look back on it, you get one shot to get

that rookie record," he said. "I came in as an unproven player in my first year and did that."[1]

He just kept on going for four teams, never thinking much about all those spectacular numbers he was putting up.

"Records are nice, but they really don't mean a lot," Dickerson said. "The minute I set one, I figure it's just there for me or somebody else to break."[2]

Unhappy with his Rams contract, Dickerson asked to be traded in 1987. He'd already scored 55 touchdowns rushing, run for more than 7,000 yards, and led the team to four straight playoff berths when he was dealt to Indianapolis. The once-lowly Colts went on to win the AFC East with Dickerson in the backfield.

Through 1989, Dickerson was on pace to easily set the NFL career rushing mark. But his running style wound up shortening his stay in the NFL.

A tall, upright runner, Dickerson took many hard hits to his legs, hips, and ribs. By his tenth season, he'd begun slowing down, and in 1992, he was traded to the Raiders, where Dickerson lasted one year. He finished as a part-timer with Atlanta for one season.

Even with those unproductive seasons late in his career, Dickerson remains one of the best and most original runners football has ever seen.

The one thing that eluded Dickerson was a championship ring.

"No, I never made it to a Super Bowl," he said when he was chosen for the Hall of Fame. "For me, this shows I did do something right in my sport."[3]

ERIC DICKERSON

BORN: September 2, 1960, Sealy, Texas.

HIGH SCHOOL: Sealy High School, Sealy, Texas.

COLLEGE: Southern Methodist University.

PRO: Los Angeles Rams, 1983–1987; Indianapolis Colts, 1987–1991; Los Angeles Raiders, 1991–1993; Atlanta Falcons, 1993.

HONORS: NFL Rookie of the Year (NFC), 1983. Pro Football Hall of Fame, 1999.

TONY DORSETT

TONY
DORSETT

The Dallas Cowboys were in a deep hole. It was the last game of a season shortened by a players' strike, and they didn't want to go into the playoffs off a loss.

But here they were at Minnesota's Metrodome. The sound from the crowd was deafening, because the Cowboys were at their 1-yard line, and their star runner, Tony Dorsett, almost missed the handoff from quarterback Danny White.

That was very unlike Dorsett. In college, he was so spectacular he set eighteen NCAA records, including rushing for 6,082 yards in four seasons, a mark that lasted for twenty-two years. The fast, shifty, and and durable Dorsett moved into the NFL and gained at least 1,000 yards in each of his first five pro seasons. In 1977, he was the NFL's Offensive Rookie of the Year and helped the Cowboys win the Super Bowl.

On this play against the Vikings' "Purple People Eaters" defense, Tony was in trouble. And then, in a flash, he was gone.

Dorsett got control of the ball, slipped through the line up the middle, cut to the right sideline, and sped 99 yards for a touchdown. It was the longest run in NFL history and always will be—unless the league lengthens the field.

"Being in the record book with a record that can never be broken, that's a good feeling," Dorsett said before his 1994 induction into the Pro Football Hall of Fame.[1]

Dorsett gave Cowboys fans good feelings for 11 years as one of pro football's great playmakers. Then he spent his final season with the Denver Broncos.

He had eight 1,000-yard seasons, scored 90 touchdowns, including 13 in the playoffs, and was the man every opponent focused on stopping.

Pretty good for a "squirt" who, as a kid, loaded up his pockets with rocks, hoping to get his weight high enough to let him play youth football. "Everybody said I'd be too small to play pro football at 188 pounds," Dorsett said with a smile. "I don't think I was too small, do you?"[2]

Dorsett grew up in western Pennsylvania, where such all-time NFL stars as Joe Montana, Joe Namath, and Mike Ditka came from. He stayed close to home in college, attending the University of Pittsburgh, leading the Panthers to a 12-0 record and the 1976 national championship—their first in thirty-nine years. He was selected first overall in the NFL draft by Dallas.

And the top is where Dorsett carried them nine months later.

"If we always run to daylight, we can always find our way back home," Dorsett said. "I'm living proof of that."[3]

TONY DORSETT

BORN: April 7, 1954, Aliquippa, Pennsylvania.

. . . .

HIGH SCHOOL: Hopewell High School, Aliquippa, Pennsylvania.

. . . .

COLLEGE: University of Pittsburgh.

. . . .

PRO: Dallas Cowboys, 1977–1987; Denver Broncos, 1988.

. . . .

RECORDS: NFL Record (tie) for longest run from scrimmage, 99 yards.

. . . .

HONORS: Heisman Trophy Winner, 1976. NFL Rookie of the Year (NFC), 1977. Pro Football Hall of Fame, 1994.

. . . .

FRANCO HARRIS

FRANCO
HARRIS

Franco Harris couldn't have done anything more famous, more celebrated, or more dramatic than what he did as a rookie for the Pittsburgh Steelers.

In 1972, after an All-American career as a fullback at Penn State, Franco was a first-round draft pick of the Steelers. Pittsburgh had joined the NFL in 1933, but in most seasons since then it had a losing record. The Steelers had never won a playoff game before Harris joined them.

By the end of his Hall of Fame career, though, Harris helped bring four Super Bowl titles to the Steel City. He was the hero of

"Franco's Italian Army" rooting section. He gained 1,055 yards and scored 10 touchdowns in his first NFL season and had seven more 1,000-yard seasons and a total of 91 TDs.

But nothing meant more than the "Immaculate Reception." It is considered the greatest play in NFL history—except by Oakland Raiders fans.

"All I remember," said Bill Cowher, who was fifteen at the time and would go on to coach the Steelers for 15 seasons and win a Super Bowl, "is this city went nuts."[1]

On an icy Three Rivers Stadium field on December 23, 1972, with every seat sold—home games were blacked out on TV in those days—the Steelers and Raiders began one of the most bitter rivalries in sports history with this postseason matchup. With 1:13 to go, the Raiders held a 7-6 lead.

The Steelers reached their 40-yard line before Terry Bradshaw threw three straight incompletions. With 26 seconds left and no timeouts, Bradshaw dropped back to pass, was pressured, and rolled to his right before heaving the ball down the middle of the field to Frenchy Fuqua. As Fuqua reached for the football, defensive back Jack Tatum arrived and hit the Steeler like a runaway train.

The ball boomeranged in the air about 20 yards as Tatum and the Raiders prepared to celebrate.

But wait.

"From my training at Penn State, I knew to follow the ball . . . always go to the ball," Harris said. "Before I knew it, I had the ball. It was just a blur, a blur. The only thing

I could think of was, `Get into the end zone. Don't even attempt a field goal, just get into the end zone.'"[2]

Which Franco did after catching the ball at his shoetops.

As fans leaped from their seats and hugged each other, and players mobbed Franco, the Raiders stormed the referee, claiming it was an incompletion. The official didn't agree, and Harris was a hero forever in Pittsburgh.

Imagine that Franco Harris, one of the all-time best rushers in NFL history, first became a star as a receiver.

"It still amazes me today," Franco said.[3]

FRANCO HARRIS

BORN: March 7, 1950, Fort Dix, New Jersey.

· ·

HIGH SCHOOL: Rancocas Valley Regional High School, Mount Holly, New Jersey.

· ·

COLLEGE: Pennsylvania State University.

· ·

PRO: Pittsburgh Steelers, 1972–1984; Seattle Seahawks, 1984.

· ·

HONORS: NFL Rookie of the Year (AFC), 1972.
Most Valuable Player, Super Bowl IX.
Pro Football Hall of Fame, 1990.

· ·

CURTIS MARTIN

CURTIS
MARTIN

Curtis Martin stood at the bottom
of a seaside cliff and looked at the
200 steps to the top. Then he went
up them—at full speed.

What was the NFL's leading rusher doing
sprinting up that staircase during the off-
season in 2005? Making himself into a better
player.

That kind of work ethic and dedication
helped make Martin one of pro football's greatest running backs and an almost certain future
Hall of Fame member. Along with Barry Sanders, he is the only player to rush for at least
1,000 yards in each of his first 10 NFL seasons.

Martin wound up with 14,101 yards, fourth on the career rushing list, and 90 touchdowns playing for the New England Patriots and New York Jets. He wasn't flashy or controversial. But his teammates and coaches always could rely on Martin.

Curtis touched people on and off the football field. One day at his church in Pittsburgh, where he grew up in a dangerous neighborhood, he walked to the pulpit and told the congregation not to make any contributions that day. Instead, he was going to give gifts to his fellow worshippers. Which he did, helping make mortgage and car payments.

"The joy on the people's faces was unbelievable," said Michael Ginyard, Curtis's lifelong friend. "Because it's unheard of. That's the trailblazer that's inside of Curt's heart. He sets those paths no man has gone before."[1]

Martin was a senior at Taylor Allerdice High School before he started playing football—very late to begin a career. But he really didn't like the game much before that.

When he realized football could help him get an education and get away from the mean streets, he got very serious about the sport, earning a scholarship to the University of Pittsburgh.

An excellent player as a junior, Curtis injured his ankle in the second game of his senior year and sat out the rest of the season. That dropped him to the third round of the draft, where New England selected him.

He became a pro star right away, though, rushing for 1,487 yards and 14 touchdowns to earn Offensive Rookie of the Year honors in 1995. The next season, he scored 14 more TDs and helped the Patriots reach the Super Bowl.

After one more 1,000-yard season with the Pats, he was signed by the Jets as a free agent. He strung together seven more 1,000-yard years, capped by a league-high 1,697 yards and 12 TDs in 2004.

"That's the one individual accomplishment I'm most proud of in my entire career," he said.[2]

CURTIS MARTIN

BORN: May 1, 1973, Pittsburgh, Pennsylvania.

. . . .

HIGH SCHOOL: Taylor Allerdice High School, Pittsburgh, Pennsylvania.

. . . .

COLLEGE: University of Pittsburgh.

. . . .

PRO: New England Patriots, 1995–1997; New York Jets, 1998–2006.

. . . .

RECORDS: Fourth leading rusher at the time he retired (14,101 yards).

. . . .

HONORS: Five Pro Bowl selections (1995, 1996, 1998, 2001, 2004).

. . . .

WALTER PAYTON

WALTER
PAYTON

It is a measure of how respected Walter Payton was that he has two awards named in his honor.

The man everyone called "Sweetness" not just for the way he ran with a football but for his personality, has his name on the Walter Payton Award given to the best offensive player in college football's lower division—in which Payton played at Jackson (Mississippi) State before becoming a pro legend. And the NFL's Walter Payton Man of the Year Award is the only league award that recognizes community involvement and service, along with on-field performance.

"He was without a doubt one of the greatest

players in the history of the sport," former NFL commissioner Paul Tagliabue said when Payton died in 1999 at age 45. "Walter was an inspiration in everything he did. The tremendous grace and dignity he displayed in his final months reminded us again why `Sweetness' was the perfect nickname for Walter Payton."[1]

A rare, high first-round draft pick from a small college—fourth overall in 1975—Payton's career took off in his second season in Chicago, the first of 10 years in which he rushed for at least 1,200 yards. He also averaged 27 catches per year and scored 125 total touchdowns.

Payton was the key to the Bears' turnaround. The storied franchise was struggling before Payton joined it. But by 1985, Chicago had one of the greatest teams in football history, going 15-1 and routing three postseason opponents to win its only Super Bowl.

In 1977, the year Payton was the NFL's MVP, he set an NFL record (since broken) with 275 yards rushing against Minnesota. He also held records for most 100-yard games (77) and, of course, most yards gained on the ground (16,726) and overall (21,803) when he retired in 1988.

But it was what Payton meant to the game and to its players that is most remembered about "Sweetness."

"He paved the way for so many small schools and players, including myself, because he opened a lot of eyes," said Jerry Rice, football's all-time leading receiver.[2]

"In the long highlight reel of this life cut short, Walter Payton will always be a man in motion: breaking tackles, breaking records, clearing every obstacle in his path," President Bill Clinton said.[3]

An emotional man, Payton lost a bet to the other members of his 1993 Hall of Fame class when he was the first to cry during the ceremonies. His son Jarrett, then 12 and a future NFL runner, introduced his father.

"After getting up here and hearing my son talk, I don't care if I lose the bet," said Payton, a winner at everything else.[4]

SWEETNESS
34

WALTER PAYTON

BORN: July 25, 1954, Columbia, Mississippi.

HIGH SCHOOL: Columbia High School, Columbia, Mississippi.

COLLEGE: Jackson State College.

PRO: Chicago Bears, 1975–1987.

HONORS: NFL Most Valuable Player, 1977.Pro Football Hall of Fame, 1993.

BARRY SANDERS

BARRY
SANDERS

One opponent said trying to tackle Barry Sanders was like trying to grab a snake soaked in grease.

Another said Sanders had two kinds of moves: unbelievable and beyond unbelievable.

Sanders used those fakes and jukes—and great speed, power, and vision—to win the 1988 Heisman Trophy at Oklahoma State. And in the NFL, Barry got even better, running his way into the Hall of Fame.

"The best football player I've ever watched was Lawrence Taylor, and the best running back I've seen in 25 years is Barry Sanders," said Matt Millen, who won four Super Bowls as a linebacker. "It's not even close. It's going to be a long, long time before we see another like him, if we do."[1]

If we do. Sanders stood only 5-foot-8, 203 pounds, but he towered above nearly every other running back in football history. Chosen third in the 1989 draft, he led the Lions to the NFC championship game in 1991.

Sanders made the Pro Bowl all-star game in all 10 of his NFL seasons, rushing for at least 1,000 yards in each year—the first player to do it. In fact, he gained at least 1,100 yards in all of those years, including 2,053 in 1997, the third most ever. Sanders had at least 100 yards in a record 14 straight games that year and led the league in rushing for the fourth time. But it was the way Sanders did it that people remember best.

"Sometimes, Barry would look like he was trapped," said Lomas Brown, a tackle for the Lions and main blocker for Sanders. "And he lost yards on some runs. But most of the time, he'd be back there and would make two, three guys miss. He'd run for 15 or 20 yards, we'd get back to the huddle and we'd all be shaking our heads like, 'How'd you do that?'"[2]

Sanders carried the ball on 3,062 NFL plays and caught 352 passes. After the 1998 season, he stood second to Walter Payton's career rushing record by 1,457 yards—fewer than Barry rushed for in '98.

With another good season, he would be the greatest of all running backs statistically. But Barry walked away—retiring just after his 31st birthday, still in his prime.

Emmitt Smith, who eventually would break Payton's

mark, admitted Sanders would have moved the record even beyond Smith's reach.

But records didn't matter to Barry. He had simply had enough of football.

"No, it never crossed my mind as a player," he said of the record. "My biggest achievement was just being able to suit up and play in the NFL. Getting to the Hall of Fame is second. It's the royalty of football and it's a tremendous and humbling honor to go in and be in the same class with the greats of our game."[3]

BARRY SANDERS

BORN: July 16, 1968, Wichita, Kansas.

HIGH SCHOOL: North High School, Wichita, Kansas.

COLLEGE: Oklahoma State University.

PRO: Detroit Lions, 1989–1998.

HONORS: Heisman Trophy Winner, 1988. NFL Rookie of the Year (NFC), 1989. Pro Football Hall of Fame, 2004.

EMMITT SMITH

EMMITT
SMITH

Already a three-time Super Bowl champion and headed for the pro football career rushing record, Emmitt Smith had reached most of his goals. Not all of them.

So the star running back for the Dallas Cowboys and 1993 NFL Most Valuable Player went back to college.

In May 1996, less than five months after earning his third championship ring, Smith earned his degree from the University of Florida.

"I'm just as thrilled about this accomplishment as I am about any other accomplishment I have achieved over the past six years," said Smith.[1]

Smith was one of the Cowboys' "Triplets," along with quarterback Troy Aikman and receiver Michael Irvin. Smith, who left the game in 2004, was a leader of Dallas's turnaround in the early 1990s from NFL weakling to Super Bowl winner. Both Aikman and Irvin say he was the best player they ever teamed with.

The 1990 Offensive Rookie of the Year, Smith led the NFL in rushing the next three years. In 1993, he was the MVP of the Super Bowl win over Buffalo.

Smith was known for his quick cuts, thick legs that allowed him to break tackles, and for his toughness. Rarely could one defender tackle him alone.

"A great thing about Emmitt was you never got a clean shot on him," said Dan Reeves, who guided the Broncos and Falcons to Super Bowls as a coach. "Only the best runners are able to do that."[2]

Smith's most memorable game was the 1993 season finale at the New York Giants. He gained 229 total yards on 32 rushes and 10 catches and scored a touchdown despite a separated right shoulder that sometimes forced his arm to hang useless at his side. The Cowboys' 16–13 overtime win clinched the NFC East and launched Dallas toward a second straight championship.

"I don't know if it was my greatest game," Smith said, "but it was one of the most important and one of the best because of what I did under those circumstances."[3]

Just as special as Smith's record 18,355 yards rushing, 3,224 yards receiving, and 183 career touchdowns was the classy way he played. When he joined the Cowboys,

Smith wrote a list of goals, and at the top was breaking Walter Payton's career rushing mark. Years before Emmitt passed that mark, the ill Payton himself asked Smith to look after his son, Jarrett, who eventually would make the NFL years after his father's death.

"E, I want you to do me a favor," Walter Payton told Emmitt Smith. "I want you to just talk to him and try to be there for him as much as you possibly can."[4]

Smith was, just as he was there whenever the Cowboys needed him.

EMMITT SMITH

BORN: May 15, 1969, Pensacola, Florida.

HIGH SCHOOL: Escambia High School, Pensacola, Florida.

COLLEGE: University of Florida.

PRO: Dallas Cowboys, 1990–2002; Arizona Cardinals, 2003–2004.

RECORDS: NFL's all-time leading rusher with 18,355 yards; most career touchdowns rushing (164); most 100+ yards rushing games (78).

HONORS: NFL Most Valuable Player, 1993. Eight Pro Bowl Selections (1990–1995, 1998, 1999).

LADAINIAN TOMLINSON

LADAINIAN
TOMLINSON

Stylish. That's the word usually used to describe LaDainian Tomlinson. Along with graceful, skilled and artistic.

Tomlinson is considered the model modern running back. He runs hard but smart, never allowing defenders to get a solid hit. He's quick enough to burst through holes or run to the outside. His hands are strong yet soft, meaning he holds onto the ball and also is a fine receiver.

Plus, he's a terrific teammate, a guy who tries his best every play, and speaks up when he believes the Chargers need a spark.

When many Chargers were forced from their

homes because of wildfires in the San Diego area in October 2007, Tomlinson showed his leadership. After leaving his house—it wound up not being touched by the fires—Tomlinson made sure the other players were safe and prepared to handle being displaced.

"We're family and it's something you do for your family," Tomlinson said.[1]

Ever since being drafted out of TCU in the first round (fifth overall) in 2001, Tomlinson has been the man in San Diego. He started every game in which he played in his first seven seasons, leading the NFL in rushing in 2006 and 2007. In '07, the Chargers made the AFC championship game; L.T.'s damaged knee limited him to two plays in that loss to the Patriots.

L.T. set 13 NFL records in 2006, including scoring 31 touchdowns (28 rushing) and 186 points. He was the league's MVP that year, when he also was selected the NFL's Man of the Year. The only thing missing in his career is a Super Bowl win.

"I don't think you necessarily need it, but it's definitely a great thing to have on your resume," he said of winning the Super Bowl. "We're on the cusp of doing something special. Special is doing something that no team in the history of the Chargers has ever done, and we've got to go put in the work to do that."[2]

Not that work has ever scared Tomlinson. When he was in college, his coaches said no one at TCU trained longer or harder. Same thing when Tomlinson joined the

Chargers; he spends more time in the weight room than most players, let alone running backs.

"He's just one of those guys who's going to continue to be the backbone of this team," said Chargers president Dean Spanos. "He's the heart and soul of this team. Like everybody says, he's as good off the field as he is on the field."[3]

LADAINIAN TOMLINSON

BORN: June 23, 1979, Rosebud, Texas.

HIGH SCHOOL: University High School, Waco, Texas.

COLLEGE: Texas Christian University.

PRO: San Diego Chargers, 2001–.

RECORDS: NFL Record for single-season touchdowns (31), rushing touchdowns (28), and most points scored in a single season (186).

HONORS: Five Pro Bowl selections (2002, 2004, 2005, 2006, 2007).

CHAPTER NOTES

CHAPTER 1. JEROME BETTIS

1. Author interview, Denver, Colorado, January 22, 2006.
2. Ibid.
3. Associated Press, Detroit, Michigan, January 30, 2006.
4. Ibid.

CHAPTER 2. JIM BROWN

1. "Athletes of the Century," Associated Press, December 9, 1999.
2. "Bock's Score," Associated Press, November 29, 1986.

CHAPTER 3. ERIC DICKERSON

1. "Dickerson Gets His Due," *Los Angeles Times*, January 30, 1999.
2. Associated Press, Anaheim, California, November 22, 1986.
3. "Dickerson Gets His Due," *Los Angeles Times*, January 30, 1999.

CHAPTER 4. TONY DORSETT

1. Hall of Fame, Canton, Ohio, Associated Press, August 1, 1994.
2. Author interview, New Orleans, Louisiana, January 24, 1997.
3. Hall of Fame, Canton, Ohio, Associated Press, August 1, 1994.

CHAPTER 5. FRANCO HARRIS

1. "Immaculate Facts," Associated Press, December 20, 1997.
2. Ibid.
3. Author telephone interview, January 29, 1990.

CHAPTER 6. CURTIS MARTIN

1. Associated Press, "Selfless Martin," Hempstead, New York, September 7, 2005.
2. Ibid.

CHAPTER 7. WALTER PAYTON

1. "The Life and Times of Walter Payton," *Chicago Tribune*, November 2, 1999,
2. Author telephone interview, July 31, 1993.
3. "Sweetness in Action," *USA Today*, November 2, 1999.
4. Pro Football Hall of Fame transcript, Canton, Ohio, July 31, 1993.

CHAPTER 8. BARRY SANDERS

1. Associated Press, "Hall of Fame-Sanders," Detroit, Michigan, August 5, 2004.

2. Author's telephone interview, July 30, 2004.
3. Author interview, Canton, Ohio, August 8, 2004.

Chapter 9. Emmitt SMITH

1. Associated Press, "Emmitt Graduates," Gainesville, Florida, May 4, 1996.
2. Author telephone interview, October 20, 2004.
3. Associated Press, "Sports Showcase," Irving, Texas, October 22, 2002.
4. Associated Press, "Jarrett and Emmitt," Coral Gables, Florida, October 31, 2002.

Chapter 10. LaDainian TOMLINSON

1. Author telephone interview, October 30, 2007.
2. Associated Press, "Chargers-Tomlinson," San Diego, California, September 6, 2007.
3. Ibid.

Further READING

Sullivan, George. *Power Football: The Greatest Running Backs*. New York: Atheneum, 2001.

Stewart, Mark and Mike Kennedy. *Touchdown: The Power and Precision of Football's Perfect Play*. Minneapolis, MN: Millbrook Press, 2010

Internet ADDRESSES

The Official Site of the National Football League
  http://www.nfl.com

Pro Football Hall of Fame
  http://www.profootballhof.com